Three Short Anthems
No. 2

God, who made the earth and sky

*An anthem or introit for Christmastide, or
for a feast of Our Lady*

by
Francis Grier

Music Department
OXFORD UNIVERSITY PRESS
Oxford and New York

God, who made the earth and sky

Text from the Stanbrook Abbey Hymnal

FRANCIS GRIER

It is left to the discretion of the performers whether some or all of the opening three verses (bars 1-15) should be sung by soli, tutti, or semi-chorus. If a decision is made in favour of smaller forces it may then also be advisable to reduce from tutti to the same forces for the last few bars of the piece (from the 4th beat, Tenor part, in b. 19). The style should be simple, flexible, and expressive.
This piece is No. 2 of Francis Grier's Three Short Anthems.

6

ISBN 978 0 19 343163 8